Original title:
The Sweetness Within

Copyright © 2025 Creative Arts Management OÜ
All rights reserved.

Author: Tobias Sterling
ISBN HARDBACK: 978-1-80586-319-9
ISBN PAPERBACK: 978-1-80586-791-3

Mirthful Reflections

In a world where giggles grow,
Ice cream mountains start to flow.
Lollipops dance with glee and flair,
Candy-coated dreams fill the air.

Jellybeans jump with silly zest,
Marshmallow clouds in a fluffy nest.
Silly hats and mismatched shoes,
Laughter glimmers like morning dew.

Savoring Simplicity

A cookie jar with a wobbly lid,
Hiding treasures, oh what a kid!
Sprinkles topple, rainbow delight,
Every bite a funny sight.

Chocolate whispers, don't you dare,
Steal a taste, if you can share!
Banana peels slip on the floor,
Giggles erupt, who could ask for more?

Hues of Happiness

Sunshine yellow, vibrant and bright,
Gummy bears bouncing in sheer delight.
Blueberry skies and cherry trees,
Tickling laughter in the breeze.

Giggles pop like popcorn loud,
Candy colors draw a crowd.
Silly socks with polka dots,
Joyful chaos in tangled knots.

Trails of Candy

Follow the path of candy dreams,
Where licorice rivers swirl in creams.
Gingerbread houses snugly sit,
With gumdrop roofs, they sure are lit.

Lollipop flowers bloom with cheer,
Honeyed whispers tickle the ear.
Marzipan critters skip and hop,
Making sure the fun won't stop.

Radiance in Shadows

In the corner, candies gleam,
Chasing shadows, like a dream.
Lollipops dance in the night,
Giggles echo with delight.

Peanut brittle sings a tune,
In the attic, with the moon.
Cookies whisper from the jar,
Sprinkled magic, near and far.

Hidden Treasures

Under cushions, snacks unfold,
Like a pirate's chest of gold.
Chocolate bars and gummy bears,
Adventures written in our chairs.

Sneaky bites, when no one sees,
Peeking out from behind the peas.
Sour treats and toffee swirls,
Sweet conspiracies of boys and girls.

The Flavor of Tomorrow

Tomorrow's tastes tucked away,
Fuzzy peaches go astray.
Whiskers twitch with hope and flair,
Hoping for a sweet affair.

Marshmallow clouds float on high,
Life is better with a pie.
Spritzers fizz with joyful cheer,
Counting munchies, never fear!

Sweet Serenade

In the kitchen, songs arise,
Cinnamon dreams and apple pies.
Baking giggles fill the air,
With a sprinkle of good care.

Peachy snacks on sunny days,
Laughter follows all our plays.
Syrup rivers, chocolate streams,
Life's a feast, or so it seems!

Beneath the Chocolate Cover

Underneath a cocoa cloak,
A hidden giggle starts to poke.
Marshmallow fluff in my right hand,
Cotton candy dreams, oh so grand.

With every bite, laughter erupts,
Chocolate rivers, oh how they erupt!
Fudge puddles where no one can see,
Joyful whispers, just you and me.

Candied Reflections of the Soul.

Jellybeans dance on my tongue,
Singing songs that I once sung.
Lollipop days, I reminisce,
Honeycomb hugs, pure bliss.

Gummy bears bear all my dreams,
In sugar-coated, silly themes.
Sippin' syrup, life feels bright,
Let's frolic in this tasty fright.

Nectar of the Soul

A sassy sip of fruity cheer,
Brings a smile from ear to ear.
Peachy giggles, lemon zest,
Every drop, it's just the best!

In this cup, joy takes a dive,
Spilling laughter, oh what a vibe!
Pineapple shouts with swirly flair,
Brightened moments float in the air.

Honeyed Whispers

Buzzing bees sing sweetly low,
As golden dreams begin to flow.
Sticky fingers, laughter's flair,
Every drop, a gentle dare.

Honey drips from giggly spots,
Silly tales in sugar plots.
Bumble the fun, let's not waste,
We're all here for a tasty taste!

Caramel Kisses

Sticky fingers and gooey bites,
A candy dance on wild delight.
Fingers cross for one more chew,
But my dentist surely knew!

Chocolate whispers, soft and sweet,
Sugar rush, we laugh on repeat.
Lollipops do a jig so bright,
Who knew candy could feel so right?

Secrets of the Heart

Whispers nestled in a cupcake,
Heart-shaped sprinkles on a flake.
Muffins hiding little jokes,
Watch out for those giggling folks!

Chocolate chips like secret dreams,
In the batter, laughter beams.
With each bite, the giggles roll,
Who knew dessert could charm the soul?

Symphony of Tenderness

Marshmallow clouds on a silly spree,
Fluffy notes in harmony.
Candy canes that twist and sway,
Playful tunes in a sweet ballet.

Lollies sing a high-pitched tune,
Gummy bears dancing to the moon.
A sprinkle here, a drizzle there,
Life's a concert, sweet beyond compare!

The Glow of Hope

A jellybean shines bright and bold,
Whispers of wishes waiting to unfold.
Cotton candy dreams in the air,
A sugary glow, without a care.

With every bite, a giggle sprouts,
Mirthful laughter, what it's about!
Life's a candy jar to explore,
With each crunch, we yearn for more!

Melted Chocolates and Warm Embrace

A bar of fudge, it slipped away,
It melted fast, oh what a day!
A gooey trail on my new shirt,
My friends just laughed, they called it art.

Chocolate chips like little flirts,
Whispering sweet, "Won't you eat us?"
I took a bite, granted a wish,
Now my waistline is not so swish!

Honeyed Words and Soft Touches

She speaks in tones, so sweetly spun,
Her words like honey, more than fun.
Each giggle lands like syrup's drip,
   Even the bees begin to sip.

A sticky mess, my hands all goo,
When she hugs tight, she sticks like glue.
I think I'm melting from her cheer,
Sweet sticky love, I'll hold you near!

The Scent of Serene Indulgence

In a bakery's warm embrace,
The scent of cookies leaves a trace.
With flour clouds and icing spills,
The kitchen's chaos feeds the thrills.

The cake I made, it looks so round,
But, oh dear, it fell to the ground!
A sweet disaster, oh what a scene,
At least the dog says I'm a queen!

Sweetness Whispered in Shadows

In the night, a candy stash,
I tiptoe near, hoping to dash.
But whispers shout, "Not yet, not now!"
The wrappers crinkle, oh what a row!

A game of stealth, my heart's in flight,
Sneaking treats by the moon's light.
I take a bite, oh what a thrill,
Until I trip and roll down the hill!

Savoring the Hidden Treat

In the cupboard, cookies hide,
With a sprinkle of joy inside.
I chomp and munch, oh what a find,
Chocolate chips, so well-designed.

Sneaky crumbs fall to the floor,
Like treasures from a secret store.
Giggles burst with each sweet bite,
In this candy-coated delight.

Candied Moments of Joy

In the morning, cereal sings,
With marshmallows and fluffy things.
I dance around, spoon in hand,
In this sugary wonderland.

Lollipops with flavors so bold,
Stand tall like heroes, brave and gold.
Each lick brings laughter, what a treat,
In a world that's hard to beat.

Beneath the Frosted Facade

Behind the cake's glamorous show,
Lies a sponge that's soft and slow.
I dive in deep, with fork in tow,
What lies beneath? More than you know!

Frosting clouds, oh so vast,
Like a sugar-coated blast!
With every forkful, smiles do spread,
Whispering secrets that can't be said.

Glimmers of Golden Kindness

Honey drips like liquid sun,
Spread on toast, oh what fun!
I share with friends, a joy ignites,
As laughter dances on those bites.

Candy wrappers crinkle in cheer,
A treasure hunt, it's finally here!
Together we savor every crunch,
In this delightful, sweetened bunch.

Delightful Echoes

In the kitchen, a cat sprawls,
Chasing crumbs as the pancake falls.
Flour on noses, such a sight,
Who knew bacon could take flight?

Syrup rivers, sticky and sweet,
Dance in circles on joyful feet.
Granny's giggles fill the air,
Who needs dinner when snacks are fair?

Heartstrings in Harmony

A ukulele sings at noon,
While the dog hums a silly tune.
Birds join in, their notes are bright,
Even frogs leap with sheer delight!

Cookies crumbling, joy unfurls,
As sprinkles rain like colorful pearls.
Laughter echoes 'round the room,
Sweet surprises like a floral bloom.

Serendipity's Caress

Stumbled on cupcakes, oh what glee!
Baked with chaos, just for me.
Jelly spills and frosting fights,
Sugar rushes ignite the nights!

Whimsical woes, flour on the floor,
Every bite opens a new door.
The mixer's dancing, what a twirl,
Catching sprinkles, what a whirl!

A Spoonful of Magic

With a spoon, I stir up cheer,
A pot of laughter, it's quite clear.
Gummy bears float in a stew,
Oh, what mischief they can do!

Whipped cream clouds cover my face,
My kitchen's a wild, happy place.
Taste-testers giggle, each in tune,
As we feast under the bright, full moon.

Cupcake Wishes

In the bakery of dreams, I seek,
With frosting smiles, oh so cheek!
A sprinkle here, a cherry there,
Sugar rush, it's all unfair!

Laughter wafts like buttercream,
In a world that feels like a meme.
Cakes in hats, a silly sight,
Who knew sweets could cause such delight?

Every bite a giggle fits,
Chocolate sprinkles, candy bits.
A cupcake called the joker's jest,
In frosting worlds, we are the best!

So grab a treat and take a bite,
Let sugary wishes take their flight.
In icing laughter, we indulge,
Come, join the scrumptious fun with bulge!

Nectar of Life

Buzzing bees in a hive of cheer,
Mixing up their honey near.
A tablespoon of silly swirls,
Making soup of snickers, twirls!

Life's a smoothie, blend it right,
With silly fruits, oh what a sight!
Bananas wearing party hats,
Bouncing berries, chatty brats!

Slurping juice, with goofy glee,
A dance-off 'tween lunch and tea.
Citrus jokes in every squeeze,
It's the nectar that aims to please!

So lift your glass, toast to the fun,
With fruity laughter, we just won.
In zesty moments, let us thrive,
In the juiciest ways, we come alive!

Melodies of Wonder

In the kitchen, pots compose,
A symphony of chef's best prose.
Singing spoons and dancing forks,
Twirling pasta, and knobby corks!

A ukulele for my pie,
As cookies croon and muffins sigh.
To bake a tune is pure delight,
With peanut butter, take a flight!

Jelly beans form a quirky band,
With candy canes that take a stand.
Sugar plums in a happy waltz,
A sweet serenade—no faults!

So gather 'round for cookie time,
As every morsel sings a rhyme.
In sugary notes, we find our cheer,
Melodic bites, oh, how they steer!

Whispers of Bliss

Hushed whispers float through pastry air,
Where cupcakes hide with little flair.
A donut giggles, a muffin winks,
In this realm, everyone thinks!

Chocolate dreams in frosted waves,
Chasing crumbs like joyful knaves.
Giggling scones, in cozy nooks,
Whispers of bliss in recipe books!

With every snack, a chuckle waits,
A comedy troupe of tasty plates.
So grab a cookie, pull up a chair,
In cheesy banter, we all share!

Through buttery breezes, joy abounds,
In sugary laughter, love surrounds.
With each delicious, silly bite,
Whispers of bliss soar to new heights!

Soft Embrace

There once was a hug, quite snug and tight,
It squeezed out the frown, brought smiles to the night.
With a squish and a squash, like jelly on toast,
You'd laugh and you'd giggle, now that's what counts most!

A blanket so warm, it snatched all your woes,
It tickled your toes, made you laugh from your nose.
Each cuddle a riddle, full of warmth and cheer,
In a world of soft chaos, you'd want to stay near.

Petals of Joy

A flower with petals, so bright and so pink,
Tried dancing with bees, but they just wouldn't wink.
It twirled in the sun, in a humor-filled spin,
And the gardener just laughed, as they fell in a bin!

Mice came to nibble the leaves, they agreed,
Who needs a bouquet when you've got a good seed?
With petals like laughter, and colors that sing,
It's the jokes in the garden that make growing a thing.

The Essence of Caring

A mug of warm cocoa, with marshmallows tall,
Made friends with a cinnamon, oh, what a ball!
They danced on the table, in a sweet little show,
While giggles erupted from the cookies below.

When a cupcake saw sprinkles, it laughed with delight,
'I'm the life of the party! The frosting just might!'
With kindness a-baking, they filled up the air,
It's the sweetness of cheer that they all like to share.

Whimsical Journeys

Off went a donut, on a journey so grand,
With a coffee companion, they formed quite the band.
They rolled down the hill, in a sugary race,
And stopped for a moment to savor the space.

A cupcake hopped by, with a sprinkle parade,
They laughed and they danced through the warm, sunny glade.
On this whimsical quest, with giggles and glee,
It's the sweetness of laughter that sets our hearts free.

Echoes of Laughter

In the kitchen, a muffin sings,
Flour fights back, oh, what fun it brings!
Sugar sprinkles jump and dance,
A whisk's wild spin, a floury romance.

Butter melts, a slippery slide,
Eggshells crack, nowhere to hide!
The timer dings, oh, hear it shout,
'Taste me now! I'm what life's about!'

Giggles burst like popcorn pop,
Baking battles, who will flop?
With laughter sweet, we can withstand,
Even burnt cookies, all laughed and planned.

Blooming Hopes

Petunias prance in sunshine bright,
Twirling petals, such a sight!
Bees buzz in a dizzy whirl,
Pollen party, around they swirl!

Gardening gloves, a fungal mess,
We dug too deep, I must confess!
But with each seed, we sow some cheer,
Waiting for flowers bright and clear.

The compost pile whispers tales,
Of worms wearing their funny veils!
In muddy shoes, we laugh and leap,
Through blooming hopes, our hearts will keep.

Flavor of Friendship

Ice cream scoops, a mountain high,
Whipped cream clouds in a blue sky!
We share a cone, both sides licked clean,
Giggles spill like melted cream.

Sour patches and gummy bears,
Jellybeans dancing in our chairs!
Let's stir the soup of silly tales,
Where every friend's a ship that sails.

Soda pop and a fizzy cheer,
Shared laughter, our favorite beer!
Taste buds tickled, hearts in sync,
Friendship's flavor—oh, what a stink!

Lush Landscapes of Laughter

Fields of giggles, rolling green,
Where pranks grow wild, a funny scene!
The cows wear hats, the sheep do play,
In this lush land, we spend the day.

Frogs on logs croak silly songs,
While crickets tap on bongo bongs!
The trees whisper secrets of glee,
As we dance like leaves in a spree.

Picnic spreads and cartoon vibes,
Silly ants in their tiny tribes!
In laughter's land, we stumble and roll,
Creating landscapes that feed the soul.

Petals and Honey

In a garden where bees dance,
Petals giggle, they take a chance.
Gnats wear glasses, buzzing quite bold,
Telling secrets, I've been told.

Bees in tuxedos, sipping their tea,
And ladybugs jive, sipping so free.
Sunflowers laugh with a twist of glee,
Winking at daisies, just wait and see.

Butterflies wear polka-dot shoes,
Flitting around like they just can't lose.
Roses join in with a twirl and a spin,
Who knew chaos could be such a win?

Sipping nectar from cups made of leaves,
Making fun of the ones who believe.
In this paradise buzzing with cheer,
Even the worms clap, it's loud and clear!

Whimsical Moments

A squirrel in a hat steals the show,
Cracking nuts while putting on a glow.
He juggles acorns, oh what a feat,
While chatting with ants, oh what a treat!

Clouds wear pajamas, drifting so slow,
Tickling the sun with a fluffy hello.
Rainbows dance in polka-dot attire,
Sipping on sunshine, they never tire.

A turtle in shades, with swagger so sly,
Calls out to a rabbit, 'Hey you! Let's fly!'
They race to the finish, a hilarious sight,
As bumblebees cheer, buzzing with delight.

Every moment here is tinged with fun,
As stars burst out when the day is done.
In this realm where laughter is key,
Whimsy reigns, wild and free!

Silken Hues

Colors spin like a merry-go-round,
In a splashy world, laughter is found.
A paintbrush tickles the canvas so bright,
Creating a party with every swipe of light.

The reds do a tango, the blues play chess,
While yellows and greens shout, 'We're the best!'
Purples wear crowns, sparkling with glee,
While oranges giggle, 'Look at me!'

Each drop of paint tells a silly jest,
Crafted with joy, we're on a quest.
Splashes and drips flow free as a kite,
In a whimsical dance under the moonlight.

Chasing rainbows, they laugh and they cheer,
With colorful dreams that draw us near.
Art is a canvas, bright and absurd,
Where every stroke laughs, no need for a word!

Taste of Dreams

A cupcake castle, frosted with joy,
Gummy bears play, oh what a toy!
Chocolate rivers and licorice trees,
Candy corn clouds float by with a breeze.

Soda pop fountains bubble and fizz,
While licorice snakes dance, what a whiz!
Marshmallow moons shine down on this feast,
Every sweet moment brings laughter, at least!

A cookie with glasses reads a tall tale,
Popcorn kernels ride a gummy whale.
Donuts wear hats, having a blast,
In this delicious world, fun contrasts!

When cupcakes giggle and brownies sing,
Joy fills the air, causing hearts to swing.
With laughter and sweetness, dreams take flight,
In the land where dessert rules the night!

Essence of Quiet Bliss

In a world of jellybeans,
I lost my way to school.
A rainbow on my shoelace,
Turned my journey into drool.

A cupcake in my backpack,
With sprinkles like confetti.
Each step a custard blast,
My feet felt light and petty.

With laughter in my pocket,
And fudge beneath my hat,
Every chance encounter,
Had me giggling like a cat.

So if you seek that bliss,
In flavors soft and sweet,
Just follow candy footsteps,
And dance on wobbly feet.

Sugar-Coated Secrets

Whispers made of bubblegum,
Float above the morning dew.
Conversations turn to sugarplums,
And secrets shared in fondue.

A gummy bear conspiracy,
Hiding right beneath my bed.
They giggle at the mystery,
And hear what's left unsaid.

In chocolate-coated mornings,
We plot a sweet parade.
Marshmallow clouds are forming,
While pancake dreams are made.

So spill your gummy secrets,
Share chocolate covered fun,
Life's a treat with laughter,
When we play, we've surely won.

Heartstrings Woven in Caramel

My heartstrings pull like licorice,
Tangled in a puddle of cheese.
When friends share tales of furbish,
Each story tops with laughter's tease.

With caramel hugs and kisses,
We twirl like sugar on a stick.
Life's punchlines are our misses,
We find the sweetest little trick.

Our laughter flows like syrup,
Sticky on our happy days.
We dance in chocolate circles,
Singing in our silly ways.

So toast to joy and chuckles,
With candy glasses raised high,
In this world of sweet giggles,
Who needs a reason why?

Beneath the Sugary Surface

Underneath the candy shadows,
Secrets stick like bubblegum.
A marshmallow table echoes,
Where laughter strikes like a drum.

With licorice ladders to climb,
And jellybean jumps galore.
Each giggle matches the chime,
Of candy hearts that implore.

In this land of frosted whims,
Life's a frolicsome delight.
With every twirl and sugar shim,
We savor joy—what a sight!

So dive into the spice of fun,
Glazed in vivid colors bright.
Beneath it all, we're just spun,
In a whirl of pure delight.

Crescendo of Sugary Laughter

In a kitchen where chaos reigns,
Sugar spills like falling rain,
A cake danced, wobbled, and popped,
Will it rise, or will it flop?

Frosting splatters on my nose,
Like confetti from a prankish rose,
Giggling at my sweet-faced mess,
Who knew baking could be such stress?

Whisking egg whites, what a sight,
My dog's a fan of the fluffy fight,
Soon we'll host a dessert parade,
With cookies in sunglasses made!

Laughter echoes through the room,
As flour fills the air with gloom,
But beneath the sugary clutter,
Our hearts blend in creamy flutter!

Beneath Layers of Frosting

Beneath the colorful icing spread,
Lies a mischief that's never dead,
A hidden wink in every bite,
Makes each taste a playful flight.

Splat! My spatula meets the wall,
Will anyone see my sugary sprawl?
Glimmers of laughter, sprinkles collide,
In this confectionery joyride!

Every layer hides a joke or two,
A pinch of chaos in every view,
When brownies dance upon the plate,
I chuckle softly, feeling great.

With every slice, a giggle bursts,
Delightful chaos, quenched thirsts,
Under frosting, we come alive,
In this kitchen, we thrive and jive!

A Garden of Hidden Flavors

In a garden where sweets take flight,
Gummy worms hold a playful bite,
Candy flowers bloom so bright,
Who needs an ordinary sight?

Marshmallow bunnies leap with glee,
While chocolate trees sway, can you see?
Sugar-cane fences, so divine,
Lemonade fountains, pure sunshine!

Every corner's a delightful tease,
Honey bees buzz with sticky ease,
With laughter trailing in their wake,
Plucking treats from our favorite lake.

Whimsy blooms in every glance,
Ready to take the sweetest chance,
In this magical treat-filled land,
Fun and flavors, oh so grand!

Lattice of Sweetened Memories

In a lattice woven with laughter's thread,
Each moment a sprinkle where joy is bred,
Crepes stacked high, a daring feat,
Here memories dance, oh so sweet!

Old family tales pour like fondant,
Sticky with giggles, deliciously haunting,
As crumbs scatter, we reminisce,
What a sugared, playful bliss!

We'll remember the pie that slipped and fell,
And splattered icing rings, oh so swell,
Every dessert bears a story to tell,
As we munch and laugh, all is well.

In this kitchen where we all unite,
Creating memories, what a delight,
Laughter and sweets, a perfect pair,
In the lattice of love, joy fills the air!

Blossoms of Gratitude

In a garden of socks, I found a shoe,
Thankful for laughter, and my dog named Drew.
He chases his tail with a curious glance,
While I just sit back, enjoying the dance.

Each cup of coffee spills tales of delight,
Sugar and cream make mornings just right.
I raise my mug high, toast to my chair,
For supporting my dreams, it's only fair.

The cat thinks it's grand, this routine we share,
Knocking down books like she just doesn't care.
A playful reminder, life's full of cheer,
In every small moment, joy is so near.

So here's to the giggles, the stumbles we make,
For finding pure joy in each tiny mistake.
With blossoms of gratitude planted all around,
We laugh through the chaos, and love what we've found.

Unseen Flavors

I stirred the pot, expecting a treat,
But tasted the spatula—oh, what a feat!
A mishmash of spices, a dash of surprise,
Unseen flavors dance right before my eyes.

Beneath the mishaps, a banquet unfolds,
With burnt toast and jam that never gets old.
Each meal's an adventure, oh what a thrill,
As I bravely explore my culinary will.

The cat snags a fish, thinks he's a gourmet,
While I try not to trip on a noodle or stray.
The laughter of friends fills up the entire room,
Unseen flavors blossom amidst all the gloom.

So here's to the moments both silly and sweet,
To tasting life's oddities, oh how they meet!
Our banquet of blunders, served with a grin,
In the kitchen of chaos, let the fun begin!

The Charm of Innocence

With crayons and paper, she colors the sky,
A masterpiece crafted, oh my! Look, oh my!
Her giggles ring out, like bells in the breeze,
As she draws a pink dragon that tickles the trees.

Puddles become oceans where pirates can sail,
With cardboard shields and a smelly cheese trail.
Her innocence shines like a star on a flight,
As she battles the monsters beneath the twilight.

In the land of make-believe, sweetness does dwell,
With goofy old socks that she knows very well.
Each laugh is a treasure, each giggle a find,
In the charm of her world, pure joy is defined.

So let us embrace, in both laughter and cheer,
The quirky creations that make life so clear.
For within her bright eyes, the magic runs free,
In the charm of innocence, that's where we'll be.

Delight in the Mundane

Waking up grumpy, hair wild as a beast,
Coffee spills over, a humorous feast.
But there's joy to be found in the simplest things,
Like dancing with dust bunnies, oh how it sings!

Mismatched socks are the latest fashion trend,
Each a small joke that the laundry will send.
We revel in weirdness, and embrace each odd flaw,
For delight in the mundane is the best kind of law.

The microwave beeps, it's a song I adore,
While I juggle my lunch, almost drop it—oh no more!
The laughter erupts, as crumbs scatter wide,
In the chaos of trying to fit in with pride.

So let's cherish our quirks, our everyday wit,
For life's little moments are truly the hit.
In the mundane we find, with brows all a-furrow,
Delight in the simple blooms bright as a sparrow.

The Soft Murmur of Sugar Crystals

In the jar where fairies dance,
Honey drips and dreams enhance,
Lick a spoon, what a delight,
Cake on cheeks, a funny sight.

Sneeze and giggle, powdered snow,
Sprinkles flying to and fro,
Cupcakes ask for silly hats,
Elephants in party flats.

Chocolate rivers flowing wide,
While gummy bears take a ride,
Marshmallow clouds soft and round,
Everyone's lost, joy is found.

Frosting battles on the plate,
Cake is late, who can relate?
Life is sweet, a comic tale,
Sugar highs will never fail.

Whispers from a Sugar Bloom

Cupcakes giggle in the sun,
Frosting swirls, oh what fun,
Candy flowers bloom in cheer,
Laughter dancing, drawing near.

Lollipop sticks stuck in hair,
Soda streams in midair flare,
Bubbles pop with joyful glee,
Syrup rivers run to sea.

Sugar ants in silly hats,
Doing the twist with acrobats,
Caramel pools so divine,
Taffy pulls a funny line.

We're all caught in sugar's grip,
On this tasty, silly trip,
Life's a carnival of dreams,
Sweetness bursts at the seams.

Living in Sweet Reverie

Floating fluff, a cotton dream,
Marshmallow clouds burst at the seam,
Chasing cookies, crumbs in hand,
Belly laughs, we made a stand.

Bubbling soda in the air,
Chocolate chips to spare,
Sugar rush in playful race,
Sticky hands, a funny place.

Gummy worms and tangy bites,
Bouncing jellies light up nights,
Jokes and jigs with every taste,
In this world, there's no haste.

Sugar's art, a pixel show,
Pull the taffy, watch it glow,
In this land we laugh and play,
Life is sweet in every way.

A Tapestry of Sugared Threads

A tapestry of colors bright,
Cookies giggle out of sight,
Muffins murmur in delight,
Making shadows dance at night.

Lemon drops roll down the lane,
Fudge is laughing once again,
Sprinkled laughter fills the air,
Candy canes in funny wear.

Baking pies with silly glee,
Slicing smiles from A to Z,
Charming treats that take a bow,
Sugar shows us how to wow.

Whisk together fun and cheer,
Let the cupcakes persevere,
In this sweet confection's dream,
Laughter flows like whipped cream.

Candied Dreams

In a world of gummy bears,
Where licorice rivers flow,
I lost my mind to marzipan,
And danced with ginger glow.

Chocolate clouds above my head,
Sprinkle rain begins to fall,
I tripped on taffy twisted strings,
And giggled through it all.

A lollipop was my new best friend,
We shared a bubble gum,
He said, 'Life's a sweet buffet,'
With a lollipop so numb.

But sneaky gummy worms do creep,
A prank they play each night,
They whisper, 'We're your dinner,'
While I'm dreaming of delight!

Beneath the Surface

Beneath the surface, candy hides,
With jelly beans all in a row,
A secret stash of fun awaits,
In pockets where no one goes.

The licorice lizards plot and scheme,
To steal a bite of cake,
But little did they know, my friend,
I'm the queen of sugar flake.

Cotton candy clouds do tickle,
My nose, a frothy dream,
I chased a marshmallow monster,
Down a sweet and sticky stream.

Muffin tops and donut holes,
Are plotting as we speak,
They think they'll steal my happy thoughts,
But I'm far too cheeky!

Joy Lies

Joy lies in funny places,
Like cupcakes sprouting legs,
They waltz around the kitchen floor,
And giggle when it begs.

A pie that sings a silly tune,
And dances on the shelf,
We take a slice and laugh aloud,
It's joy we can't quite help.

Chocolate chip cookies plotting,
To make a tasty heist,
But when they creep up on my plate,
I know it's gonna be nice.

So here's to dessert shenanigans,
And all the tricks they play,
In a world where laughter lives,
I'm here to eat all day!

Hidden Delights

Hidden delights call my name,
Like peach pie in the sun,
I peek beneath the cookie jar,
To see what I can stun.

A donut with a wiggly grin,
Is bouncing on the shelf,
I ask, 'Are you a snack?' he says,
'No, I'm just myself!'

Brownies wrapped in mystery,
Demand I take a taste,
But oh, the giggles start to bloom,
With every single paste.

Whipped cream hidden under hats,
Of fruit that sings and sways,
The kitchen's full of fun around,
In funny, sweet displays!

Sugar-Coated Reflections

Sugar-coated reflections,
Dance on plates of gold,
They spin around the peppermint,
With stories to be told.

A marshmallow moon is glowing bright,
While gumdrops shoot for stars,
They giggle with the grape juice fairies,
In their bright, shimmering cars.

A chocolate river in a dream,
Flows sweet beneath the smiles,
Where jelly beans exchange their jokes,
And laugh across the miles.

So join this feast of silly sweets,
In every wondrous bite,
For laughter's just a sprinkle away,
In the candy-colored night!

Essence of Light

A cookie jar sits high and proud,
The lid pops off, the kids scream loud.
Chocolate chips dance, a twirl and spin,
Who knew a snack could make such a din?

Gummy bears hop, so bright and bold,
Unicorns whisper secrets of gold.
With bubbles of laughter, we munch and crunch,
Who needs a meal when you have this bunch?

Marshmallow clouds float on sugary air,
We wave to the fruit flies, without a care.
Lollipops shimmer like stars in the sky,
Every sweet bite makes our spirits fly!

At the end of the feast, we all turn round,
With hands on our bellies, joy can be found.
It's clear in this chaos where joy does reside,
In sugary moments, we always abide.

Celebrations of Serenity

Birthday hats on, we gather around,
The cake in the middle, it's too good to sound.
Candles are lit, but what's this surprise?
A frog on the frosting? Wait, is that wise?

Streamers of noodles hang from the chair,
Cheese puffs are glimmering, don't mind the glare.
We feast like kings, on snacks piled up high,
Who knew that choco-tacos could fly?

With laughter echoing against the walls,
Forget the fancy, we're here for the brawls.
A dance-off ensues, we twirl and glide,
While munching on treats, oh, what a ride!

As the day ends with a sugar rush,
We gather our treasures, in a happy hush.
Every bite a memory we can replay,
In our cozy kingdom of delightful sway.

Glistening Pathways

Lemonade stands sprout like flowers in spring,
Sipping from cups, we laugh and swing.
Ice cream trucks roll by like magic on wheels,
Every cone we devour brings giggly squeals.

Rainbow sprinkles raining down on our heads,
Chocolate rivers flow where no one dreads.
Adventure awaits with candy galore,
Each corner we turn, there's always more!

Bubblegum balloons float up to the sky,
Making wishes on flavors as they fly by.
We'll spin in the joy of all things absurd,
Where laughter is layered, and life is a curd.

With paths made of sugar, we roam free and wide,
In this whimsical world, there's nowhere to hide.
A feast for the senses, where fun's intertwined,
In this joyful journey, pure bliss we find.

Glimpses of Delight

Marshmallow trees sway in the sweet sunlight,
Candy canes peeking, oh what a sight!
Jellybeans giggle as they bounce on the grass,
In this sugary wonder, let's all raise a glass!

Cotton candy clouds drift down the lane,
In this land of delights, who feels the strain?
Sipping from puddles of bright fruity zest,
In a world full of snacks, we consider it best.

Cookies with faces, they wink and they cheer,
Whispers of frosting drift near and dear.
With every delight, our spirits will soar,
In this charming wonder, we keep wanting more!

As twilight dances, we savor each bit,
In our goofy adventures, we never quit.
For in laughter and sugar, we gleefully play,
Creating memories that won't fade away.

Flavors of Compassion

In a kitchen where laughter brews,
Spices dance in mismatched shoes.
A pinch of kindness, a dash of cheer,
Whisk away troubles, make them disappear.

Cooked up memories, oh what a treat,
With sprinkles of joy, can't be beat.
Sour faces turn sweet with a guffaw,
Taste testing friendship, the best kind of law.

Muffins shaped like silly clowns,
Watch them rise as the laughter downs.
Frosting giggles that stick like glue,
Churned by hearts, not a single boo!

So grab your spoons, let's stir the pot,
Compassion's flavors can't be bought.
A recipe penned by the lightest hands,
Served with smiles across all lands.

Mirth in the Mundane

Dust bunnies dance in the sunlight's beam,
As we vacuum and giggle, a silly dream.
The mundane tasks, oh what a show,
With each little chore, the laughter will grow.

Laundry becomes a game of toss,
Socks on our hands, now look at the gloss!
Folding shirts? A comedy script,
It's a circus act when we've got a quip!

Dishes shine bright like stars at night,
We sing while we scrub, what a delight!
So raise a glass, toast the chore we dread,
For laughter is the icing on life's bread.

In the drudgery lies the clever twist,
Find joy in the tasks that often get missed.
With giggles and grins, the work's all in fun,
Turning chores into laughter, oh what a run!

Sweetness of Solitude

In quiet corners where whispers bloom,
Chocolate thoughts swirl around the room.
Cake crumbs of silence scatter the floor,
As introspection opens the door.

Baking brownies, a solo affair,
Licking the spoon without a care.
A dash of daydreams, a sprinkle of thought,
Oh, how sweet the monsters I've caught!

Tea bags giggle in the quiet steep,
With cookie companions, a promise to keep.
The oven hums a solo tune,
As my heart swells under the lazy afternoon.

So here's to the times spent all alone,
In this sugary kingdom, I've grown my throne.
Finding joy in the stillness, the sweet and the right,
In solitude's embrace, my heart takes flight.

The Taste of Togetherness

Gather 'round the table, what a sight!
Pasta twirls and laughs in the light.
Each plate a story, freshly made,
Topped with memories, nothing can fade.

Spoons clash in harmony, forks chase cheese,
While jokes fly like bubbles on the breeze.
A pot of giggles, boiling hot,
From every person, we craft our spot.

Brownies are passed, and secrets shared,
Each slice of laughter shows that we cared.
Sauce spills over just like our tales,
United by flavor, friendship prevails.

So here's to the moments, so rich and divine,
In each tender hug and in every line.
Together we feast, with delight we confess,
It's not just the food, it's the love we possess.

Sweetly Sown Wishes

In a garden of giggles, we sow,
With wish-grains that dance, all aglow.
A sprinkle of laughter, then we grow,
Like daisies that tickle, a bright show.

Umbrellas of candy, come take the ride,
With jellybean ponies, we'll laugh and slide.
Wishing on cupcakes, what joy inside,
Come join the fun, let worries subside.

Each twinkle a wish, in this joyous spree,
With sprinkles of cheer, just you and me.
Woven in colors of pure glee,
In this world of fun, forever free.

So here's to the laughter, whimsical and true,
In our garden of wishes, we dance anew.
With hearts full of sweetness, we'll chase the blue,
Together we'll laugh, just me and you.

The Taste of Radiance

A scoop of sunshine on a waffle cone,
Laughter drips down, it's fully blown.
Flavor bombs bursting in joyous tone,
With chocolate giggles, we feel at home.

Banana peels slide in a wild swirl,
Jokes on the tip, like a topsy twirl.
Sweet whispers of jelly make our heads whirl,
In a carnival of taste, let joy unfurl.

Cotton candy clouds hang over our heads,
With each fuzzy bite, disbelief spreads.
Sipping from dreams where whimsy treads,
In a bowl of joy, our laughter spreads.

So grab a spoon, don't you dare be shy,
Taste the bright moments as they flit by.
In a world of flavors, let spirits fly,
With radiance sweet, we'll never say goodbye.

Gentle Moments

A tickle from time in a gentle breeze,
Laughing at shadows, we bend our knees.
With whispers of love in the rustle of leaves,
Each moment we share is a sweet tease.

Chasing soft clouds on a color parade,
With ice cream dreams in the cool shade.
Every giggle shared is a memory made,
In this silly dance, we're never afraid.

Holding hands with joy, we skip through the grass,
With lollipops spinning as moments pass.
Gentle and warm, like a sweet cup of sass,
In this dance of giggles, we flourish en masse.

So here's to the smiles, let worries be few,
Each moment a treasure, just me and you.
With gentle laughter, our colors renew,
In the softest embrace, forever true.

Warmth Wrapped in Kindness

A hug like a burrito, snug and tight,
Wrapped in warm kindness, oh what a sight.
With sprinkles of joy in the soft twilight,
Dancing through life, our spirits take flight.

Cupcakes with frosting, kindness like glue,
Slipping and sliding on marshmallow dew.
Each giggle a gift, a heart that grew,
In this sweet adventure, just us two.

Baking up laughter with cookies to share,
Sprinkling sugar and kindness in the air.
With warmth on our cheeks, there's plenty to spare,
In this cozy moment, no worry or care.

So here's to the hugs that keep us alive,
In this world of laughter, we genuinely thrive.
Wrapped in the warmth, together we strive,
With kindness our compass, forever we dive.

Shimmering Moments

In a jar of jellybeans found,
My cat's eyes sparkle all around.
She thinks they're toys, oh what a sight,
Chasing them under the moonlight.

A fountain of giggles, candy's delight,
Puppies dance by, oh what a fright!
They try to catch, but end up stuck,
Bouncing around like a silly duck.

Lollipops twirl in a sweet parade,
With gumdrop hats and candy made.
Listen close to the laughter's cheer,
This goofy circus is always near.

Bubbles of joy in every bite,
Sugar rushes, pure delight!
In this world where colors blend,
Every moment's a joke, my friend!

Ephemeral Joy

A flip of a coin, what will it be?
Chocolate rain or a gum tree?
Twisting my fate, with sprinkles galore,
A brief laugh leads to giggles and more.

Frogs in tuxedos jump with flair,
Stealing my candy, but I don't care!
They croak a tune, quite off the beat,
Making me laugh while they dance on my feet.

Marshmallow clouds drift in the sky,
Whipped cream dreams, oh my, oh my!
I'll float on sweetness, life's sugary game,
Writing punchlines that never feel lame.

Moments like these, so fleeting, so true,
Candy-coated giggles just for you.
I save them in jars, they sparkle and gleam,
A collection of joy, my candy-coated dream.

Candy Colored Thoughts

Skittles rain down, a vibrant show,
Each color whispers, 'Come on, let's go!'
I dream of a world where frogs wear shoes,
And chocolate rivers give me the blues.

Cotton candy clouds float with grace,
While gummy bears run a wild race.
One slows down, takes a long drink,
And out of his nose, a bubble will pink!

Cereal spoons dance in the sun,
With marshmallow warriors just having fun.
They joust with gumdrops, scatter with flair,
Making me giggle in my bright chair.

In this world of laughter, silliness sways,
Where every moment brings smiles to stay.
So grab a handful of jelly and cheer,
Playfully laugh while the world's full of cheer!

Radiant Heartbeats

A cupcake tower sways like a dream,
Each frosting swirl a sugary beam.
With cherries on top shouting, 'Hooray!',
We dance around once more in play.

Clowns juggle donuts, a comical feat,
Puppies bark at their sugary treat.
Sprinkles fly like confetti in flight,
And laughter erupts in the warm twilight.

Glazed croissants join the evening spree,
With jelly roll friends rolling with glee.
Ticklish tummies burst with delight,
As candy confetti lights up the night.

In this whimsical place of pure fun,
Every heartbeat dances, a sugary run.
So let's savor moments that quirkily shine,
For joy's a treasure, a sweet divine!

Gentle Compositions

A cat sits grinning with a pie,
Mice in tuxedos just passing by,
Laughter bubbles in the air,
As jellybeans dance without a care.

A squirrel wears glasses, reads the news,
While ducks debate their fancy shoes,
Each nut they gather, a treasure chest,
In this wacky world, life's simply the best.

Spilled lemonade on a sunny day,
Makes the ants do a funky ballet,
Giggling flowers, they're dressed to impress,
In the garden of quirks, no room for stress.

Cupcakes with sprinkles, a comedy show,
Sugar and giggles start to flow,
In every corner, laughter's a treat,
Life's a circus, oh, isn't it sweet!

Tender Footsteps

A penguin slipped on a silver skate,
With a tumble and twirl, such a funny fate,
His friends all gathered, giggling loud,
In their cool tuxedos, oh, so proud.

Bouncing bunnies hop to a beat,
Wearing top hats on their furry feet,
Each jump a question, a silly quiz,
What's the best snack? A carrot fizz!

A turtle tried dancing, oh so slow,
With a hat so big, he fell on his toe,
As laughter erupted from all around,
Joyful moments easily found.

Picnic ants with their tiny feast,
Play games of chess with a crumb as the beast,
Life is a joke, wrapped in delight,
In silly moments, all feels right!

Joy Unveiled

A snail sets sail on a candy boat,
With jellybeans as sails, afloat,
His snail friends laugh, they point and tease,
As they munch on leaves, with a gentle breeze.

Mice in pajamas, a wild dance crew,
With cheese hats on as they twirl and skew,
The cat is the DJ, spinning tunes,
As laughter echoes 'neath the dancing moons.

A circus of socks in the washing machine,
Performing acrobatics, oh so keen,
Lost in the spin, they swirl and dive,
In this fabric world, they feel alive.

Cookies at midnight, a taste of glee,
Baking in trouble, oh let it be,
Each bite a giggle, a sprinkle of fun,
In the kitchen's chaos, joy's never done!

The Flavor of Serenity

A marshmallow cloud floats in the sky,
With licorice vines and a cherry pie,
As lollipops rain down in delight,
Tickling toes under stars at night.

A cupcake party with silly hats,
Brought together by giggling chitchats,
Frosting rivers where friends all glide,
In a taste-filled world, joy can't hide.

Chocolate rivers, bridges of cream,
With gingerbread houses, life's a dream,
Sprinkled giggles from every direction,
In this sweet place, there's pure affection.

A jazzy banana plays the flute,
While pineapples dance in a funky suit,
Every moment sprinkles laughter anew,
In a world of flavor, we chase the hue.

Hidden Honeycomb

In the cupboard, jars do hide,
Filled with goodies, sweet and fried.
I take a scoop, oh what a tease,
The ants join in, they want their piece.

A sticky mess, my fingers gleam,
Licking honey, living the dream.
Scooping more, my mom will shout,
'Who ate my honey? Come on out!'

Buzzing friends, they join the feast,
A hive of laughter, never ceased.
Each taste a giggle, oh what fun,
In this sweet race, we all have won!

So here's to jars, and all their cheer,
In hidden nooks, they draw us near.
Grab a spoon, let the fun unfold,
In the sticky, sweet, and bold!

Nectar in the Heart

A little pot sits on the shelf,
I just can't keep it to myself!
With every drip, my heart takes flight,
Like candy dreams on a starry night.

I pour it gently on my toast,
A breakfast treat, I love the most.
Oh, the giggles when it spills,
A tasty chaos, what a thrill!

A spoonful swirls, a joyful dance,
I twirl around, given the chance.
Neighbors peek through window shade,
Wondering what fun I've made.

So let's embrace the sticky joy,
And be a kid, not just a boy.
In every drop, a secret part,
A little nectar in the heart.

Embrace of Sugared Whispers

In the garden, blossoms sway,
Whispers sweet lead me astray.
Tiny treasures all around,
In sugared dreams, joy is found.

Bumblebees dance without a care,
As gummy bears float in the air.
I chase them down, what a sight!
Candy clouds in the morning light.

Lemon drops, and jellybeans,
Playing tricks on my wild dreams.
Twinkling giggles with every bite,
In sugary whispers, pure delight!

So let's gather all that's sweet,
Life's a treat, can't be beat.
With every laugh, our hearts can sing,
In this embrace, we'll never cling!

Hidden Treasures of Delight

Beneath the floorboards, what do I find?
An ancient stash, delightfully unsigned!
Chocolates wrapped in crinkled foil,
A treasure trove, oh how they spoil!

I nibble here, I munch and chew,
Laughter bubbles from within, it's true!
Fudge-caked fingers, what a sight!
Can't hide the crumbs, try as I might!

Each secret bite, a giggling spree,
Sharing treats with my friend, whee!
In every bite, a taste divine,
With every laugh, our hearts entwine.

So here's to treasures, found and shared,
In hidden places, we've all dared.
With every giggle, we spread the light,
In these sweet moments, pure delight!

Joys Wrapped in Silk

In a candy store, I lost my shoe,
Dancing with gummies, oh, what a view!
Lollipops giggle, chocolate bars tease,
Marshmallow clouds drifting on a breeze.

Fudge falls on my head like a comical rain,
The laughter in circles, I can't explain.
Lollies parade on a sugar-coated road,
While I wrestle a licorice snake, oh, what a load!

Cupcakes sing songs, sprinkles in their hair,
They flirt with my frosting, but I'm not scared.
With each sugary bite, I waltz and I sway,
In this candyland chaos, I want to stay!

So here's to the fun, in every sweet treat,
In sugar-coated joy, my heart finds its beat.
Wrapped in silly dreams, with mirth all around,
In this realm of desserts, true happiness found.

The Confectioner's Dreams

Whisking in the kitchen, oh what a sight,
A bubblegum tornado takes off in flight.
With a dash of mischief and a sprinkle of cheer,
The cakes start giggling, it's party time here!

Sifting sugar like snowflakes, a powdery dance,
Brownies do the cha-cha, they're taking the chance.
A cupcake rebels, it flips and it spins,
It's a dessert revolution where laughter begins!

Pudding cups burst with jokes that they tell,
As jellybeans ponder their fate in this shell.
Chocolate rivers bubble with laughter and light,
Every sweet moment absurdly just right!

In this bakery madness, the silliness flows,
With giggles and grins as the oven door glows.
From lemon tart tales to marzipan dreams,
The confectioner's visions are brighter than beams!

Delicate Drops of Affection

Honey drips slow from a mischievous bee,
Tickling my nose like a soft jubilee.
Custard cups wink, with a playful intent,
As doughnuts conspire, their sweetness unbent.

Every bubblegum burst is a giggle divine,
Frosting on muffins, sweet battles align.
The pastry brigade has a whimsical sway,
Riding in pies on a sugary bay!

Taffy twists tumble, in hilarious loops,
While caramels plot in their gooey groups.
A macaroon skates on a sugar-frost floor,
Each nibble of laughter opens a door!

So let's raise a toast with our cocoa delight,
To the moments of joy that sparkle so bright.
In this confectionery realm, we find a connection,
With each sweetened drop, an odd affection!

Sweet Echoes in the Silence

In the pantry at night, there's a rustling sound,
A cookie jar giggles, a secret abound.
Marzipan whispers and licorice sighs,
As brownies play hide and seek in disguise!

The silence grows loud with each tiny crunch,
As sneaky delights conspire for lunch.
Cheesecakes are plotting a creamy escapade,
In a world of desserts, no plans are delayed!

Wanton chocolate bars dodge and weave,
Their pearly wrappers make me believe.
That even in quiet, fun comes alive,
With cupcakes and cookies, they joyfully thrive!

So grant me the laughter, the sweet and the small,
In this kitchen chaos, together we haul.
With echoes of giggles wrapped up in delight,
In moments of silence, we party all night!

www.ingramcontent.com/pod-product-compliance
Lightning Source LLC
Chambersburg PA
CBHW060123230426
43661CB00003B/310